TWO LECTURES

INTRODUCTORY TO THE

STUDY OF POETRY.

TWO LECTURES

INTRODUCTORY TO THE

STUDY OF POETRY

BY THE

Rev. H. C. BEECHING M.A.

LATE CLARK LECTURER AT TRINITY COLLEGE, CAMBRIDGE,
PROFESSOR OF PASTORAL THEOLOGY AT KING'S COLLEGE, LONDON,
CHAPLAIN TO THE HON. SOC. OF LINCOLN'S INN.

CAMBRIDGE:
AT THE UNIVERSITY PRESS.

1901

CAMBRIDGE
UNIVERSITY PRESS

University Printing House, Cambridge CB2 8BS, United Kingdom

Published in the United States of America by Cambridge University Press, New York

Cambridge University Press is part of the University of Cambridge.

It furthers the University's mission by disseminating knowledge in the pursuit of education, learning and research at the highest international levels of excellence.

www.cambridge.org
Information on this title: www.cambridge.org/9781107654914

© Cambridge University Press 1901

First published 1901
First paperback edition 2014

A catalogue record for this publication is available from the British Library

ISBN 978-1-107-65491-4 Paperback

PASSION AND IMAGINATION
IN POETRY.

THE unsatisfactoriness of definitions of poetry arises usually from one or other of two causes. If the definition is that of a critic, it is the resultant of a long analytical process, and therefore not very intelligible apart from the process by which it has been arrived at; if it is the definition of a poet, it is certain to contain that element of poetry which it professes to explain. Nevertheless, the most helpful *aperçus* into poetry are those which the poets themselves have given us, and of them all none is more helpful than that inspired parenthesis in which Milton one day summed up its characteristics as "simple, sensuous, and passionate."

We may presume that by his first epithet Milton intended that simplicity which is another name for sincerity. He meant that a poet must look at the world frankly and with open eyes; with the spirit, though with more than the wisdom, of a child. We sometimes express another side of the same truth by saying that poetry is "universal," meaning that it cares nothing for superficial and transient fashions, but is interested only "in man, in nature, and in human life," in their permanent elements. This first epithet seems to fix beyond dispute an indispensable quality of all poetry. If a writer is insincere, or if he is conventional and fashionable, we are sure, whatever his airs and graces, that he is no poet. By "sensuous" it is probable that Milton meant what, in more technical language, we should describe as "concrete." Poetry deals with things, and it deals with people; it sings of birds and flowers and stars; it sings of the wrath of Achilles, the wanderings of Ulysses and Æneas, the woes of

King Œdipus, the problems of Brutus and Hamlet; whatever be the thought or the emotion it is concerned with, it is concerned with them as operating on a particular occasion; it has no concern with the intellect or the emotions or the will in abstraction from this or that wise or passionate or wilful person [1]. By his third epithet Milton, as most will agree, touched, or almost touched, the heart of the matter. We all conceive prose to be an adequate vehicle for our level feelings, but as soon as we are deeply moved and wish to express our emotion we instinctively turn to the poets. Wordsworth is at one with Milton in fixing upon passion as

[1] The tradition of this concreteness was not lost even in the eighteenth century. Poets, living in a time of abstract thought, and feeling under the necessity of handling abstractions, hit upon the device of personifying them, with the result that from the pages of Dodsley's *Miscellany* every faculty of the mind and every operation of every science looks out at one with a capital letter, a fashion happily parodied in the famous line :

" Inoculation, heavenly maid, descend."

Gray is not untouched with the malady, though, on the whole, he represents a reaction back to the richness of the concrete, the " pomp and prodigality " of Shakespeare and Milton.

of the essence of poetry, which he in one place defines as "the spontaneous overflow of powerful feelings." It does not matter for poetry what the emotion is that overflows; it may be love or hate, pity or fear, awe or indignation, joy or sorrow; what matters for poetry is that some passion there should be, for some particular object, and that it should be sincerely and deeply felt.

Essential, however, as passion is, so that where there is no passion there can be no poetry, in saying passion we have not said the last word. Anyone may prove this to himself by a simple reminiscence. He may at some time have been in love, for, according to Patmore, "Love wakes men once a lifetime each"; and, perhaps, in a mood of exaltation he may have taken pen and paper for a sonnet to his mistress' eyebrow; but the poetry did not come; or, if something came, in a calmer mood he recognized that it was not poetry. Or we may illustrate from other passions. At the Queen's

Jubilee a few years since we were all passionately loyal, and the morning newspapers vied with each other in producing odes ; but no one could mistake any one of them for poetry. Or, the other day, again, when the Rennes verdict was announced, the intelligence of England was roused to a passion of indignation. I took up my weekly gazette the next Saturday morning and found that indignation had made a good many verses, in none of which was there a tincture of poetry. There was much cursing and swearing, and appealing to Heaven for vengeance ; but the point of view was merely that of " the man in the street."

These simple examples will suffice to show that poetry requires a manner of viewing things which is not that of the average man, but is individual to the poet; it requires, in a word, genius. One could hardly expect Milton to point this out ; having genius himself he would assume that everyone else had genius ; he would assume that we all had the power of looking at the world not only *frankly* but *freshly*, because he would not understand any other way of looking at it. Now, it is this fresh outlook and insight, this power of viewing things and people out of the associations in which the rest of mankind habitually view them, that is the root of the whole matter. In the world of nature we find the poets moved even to passion by objects that we hardly notice, or from long familiarity have come to ignore. Their strong emotion arises from their fresh vision. By means of that fresh vision the world never ceases to be an interesting place to them.

> " By the murmur of a spring,
> Or the least bough's rustling,
> By a daisy whose leaves spread
> Shut when Titan goes to bed,
> Or a shady bush or tree,
> She could more infuse in me
> Than all Nature's beauties can
> In some other wiser man."

So sang Wither of the Poetic Muse ; and Blake expresses the same truth in his inspired doggrel :

> "What to others a trifle appears
> Fills me full of smiles and tears."

The converse of the proposition also holds true: what to others may appear facts of the highest importance, may to the poet appear trifles. Similarly in the world of men we find the poets as much interested in the least as in the greatest, and we find them unconcerned by many of the distinctions which to mankind in general appear vital. We find, for example, Andrew Marvell introducing into his panegyric of Oliver Protector a picture of King Charles at his execution, which embalms the secret of all the cavalier loyalty, and is to-day the oftenest quoted passage of his poem.

The poet's subjects, then, are borrowed from any quarter in the whole range of nature and human experience; "the world is all before him where to choose"; anything that excites any deep emotion in him is a fit topic for his verse, and it is our privilege for the moment, so far as that one experience is concerned, to look through his eyes. In this way the poets interpret the world to us. They also interpret us to ourselves. They make adventurous voyages into hitherto unsounded seas of the human spirit, and bring us word of their discoveries. And what they thus win becomes an inalienable possession to the race ; the boundaries of humanity are pushed back. This power of interpreting the world and human life is sometimes spoken of as an idealizing faculty, and no exception can be taken to the term so long as it is not explained to mean that the poet tricks up what he sees in false lights in order to please us. For anyone who considers the best poetry, whether about the universe or man's heart,— and it is only the best that must determine the genus—will admit that, so far as he has trusted himself to it, it has convinced him of its entire veracity. It is idealized only in the sense that a landscape is idealized by the removal of the accidental and commonplace details, which sufficed to blind others to the beauty that the painter distinguished. The artist, poet or painter, sees the light that never was on sea or land until he saw it ; but when he has once seen it and shown it us, we can all see that it is there, and is not merely a figment of his fancy. This mode of viewing things, which by its freshness reveals, or interprets, or idealizes, is what is meant by Poetical Imagination.

But now that that most terrifying of technical terms has been mentioned, it may be well to make a short summary of the various senses in which the word is habitually employed, in order to observe what all or any, of them have in common, and how they connect one with another.

(*a*) When a psychologist speaks of imagination he is not thinking of poetry ; he means by the word the power of summoning again before the mind's eye vivid images of what has been once seen. He bids us look carefully at our breakfast-table, and then, closing our eyes, notice how much of it we can recall, how clear or dim an image. Whether skill in this memory-picturing has any link with poetical imagination it would be hard to say ; certainly to no one would a power of vividly recalling images be of greater service. The faculty seems to be entirely distinct from the power of attention and close observation.

(*b*) A more familiar usage of the word is that which makes it almost a synonym for sympathy—the power of projecting self into the circumstances of others. We know to our cost that many men and women are sadly to seek in this faculty, and it seems to be no especial prerogative of poets, though Shelley thought so. He speaks of the poet as—

> " A nerve o'er which do creep
> The else unfelt oppressions of the earth."

And in his prose essay he says : "A man to be greatly good must imagine intensely and comprehensively ; he must put himself in the place of another, and of many others ; the pains and pleasures of his species must become his own"; and he continues, "The great instrument of moral good is imagination, and poetry administers to the effect by acting upon the cause" (*Essays*, I. 16). Shelley in this passage is theorizing too much from his own personal feelings; for it has often been remarked that poets have been singularly lacking in imagination of this moral sort, and some have been conspicuous for an intense selfishness in their domestic relations.

(*c*) But the word is also used not of moral, but of intellectual, sympathy; a power of appreciating, by an act of intuition, the characteristic qualities of things and people so as to be able to set out a train of consequences. A celebrated novelist was once congratulated upon the admirable drawing in one of her books of a particular school of Dissenters, and she was asked what opportunities she had enjoyed of studying them. Her reply was that she had once caught sight of a group of them through a half-opened door as she mounted a staircase.

That is no doubt an extreme case, but it is all the more useful as an illustration. It helps us to realize how potent a faculty is the endowment of the dramatist, which can pierce through human appearance to its essential qualities, can conceive by a sure instinct how, in given circumstances, the given character must act, and can represent it to us, because it is vivid to him, in all the verisimilitude of essential detail. Such imagination is plainly one large and special side of the faculty of seeing things out of their commonplace associations. As a branch of the same head would rank the still rarer power of conceiving types of character, that for certain reasons have no actual existence in the world we know, such types as Shakespeare's Ariel and Caliban and Puck.

(*d*) The word imagination is also used of a faculty which may at first sight seem the opposite of this—a faculty of seeing people and objects not as they are in themselves, but coloured by the atmosphere of joy or gloom

through which they are seen. The truth, however, probably is that nothing at all is, or ever
can be, seen out of some atmosphere, a thing
in itself being merely an abstraction; but the
greater a poet is, the more various are his moods,
while with lesser men a particular mood may
cover all the objects in their poetical world.

(*e*) Again, the word has a narrower and
more technical sense; namely, the power of
detecting resemblances in nature for the purpose
of poetical illustration. This use of the term
is not merely freakish, but connects with that
broader and more fundamental sense to which
I have so many times referred, the power and
habit of seeing the "common things that round.
us lie" out of their commonplace associations,
of seeing them in more subtle and original
associations. For it is the power of bringing
together two objects or events that the ordinary
person would never dream of connecting, but in
which the poet's eye has detected similarity, and
which he therefore places side by side so that

one may throw light upon the other. Our
thinking, it will be admitted, is largely asso-
ciational; one thing recalls another; but it is
the prerogative of poets that the tracks between
idea and idea in their minds are not those of
common trade. Recur for a moment to Wither's
reference to a daisy. We know beforehand
what a daisy will suggest to a child, what to
a gardener, what to a botanist; we do not know
beforehand what it will suggest to a poet. It
may suggest, as it did to Chaucer, a crowned
queen :—

> "A fret of gold she haddë next her hair,
>   And upon that a white corown she bare
>   With flourouns smallë, and (I shall not lie)
>   For all the world right as a daïsy
>   Ycrowned is with whitë leaves light,
>   So were the flourouns of her corown white."

How utterly different from this is the vision
of Burns! To him the daisy is the type of
humble cheerfulness, sweet neighbour and meet
companion of the humble and cheerful lark.
How different, again, was the feeling it in-

spired in Wordsworth! The point to strike
home to him was the touch of kinship between
the simplest flower and man in the fact that
both are alive:

> " Sweet silent creature
> That *breath'st* with me in sun and air."

Imagination, used in this restricted sense of
the interpretation of phenomena by comparison,
is often contrasted with a weaker form of itself
to which the name of Fancy is given. The
distinction was introduced into these islands
by Coleridge, from whom it was borrowed by
Wordsworth; it was then popularized by Leigh
Hunt and afterwards by Ruskin. It has played
in the last half century so prominent a part
in the criticism of poetry, that it is perhaps
worth while to look it for once fairly in the
face. Coleridge was always promising to give
a disquisition upon Poetical Imagination, but
he never kept his word; he did, however, what
was almost better; in the *Biographia Literaria*
he illustrated his meaning from some passages

in his friend's poems; and we gather from his comments that he did not at all mean Imagination to be distinguished from Fancy as the perception of deeper from that of more superficial resemblances; he wished the term Fancy to be kept for the use of poetical imagery of all kinds, and the term Imagination to be used of the poet's faculty as a creative artist. He speaks of it as a unifying power, bringing together whatever will help his purpose, and rejecting all that is impertinent and unessential. He speaks of it also as a vivifying power, turning "bodies to spirits by sublimation strange." That is to say he uses Imagination not so much of a quality of the poet's mind as of an artistic power which he exercises, the power of imposing living form upon dead matter,—he calls it in the *Ode to Dejection* "my *shaping* spirit of imagination";—but it is not hard to see that this unifying and vitalizing power depends upon what is the characteristic essence of imagination, the unanalyzable power of seeing things freshly and in new and harmonious associations. The idea must precede the execution, and it is a small matter whether the term Imagination be employed of the idea or the embodiment. Between Imagination and Fancy, therefore, as Coleridge conceived them, there could be no confusion.

The trouble began with Wordsworth. By Imagination, as by Fancy, Wordsworth practically means the use of poetical imagery; but he ascribes to the higher faculty the images which occur to the poet not in his superficial moods, but under the influence of deeper emotion[1]. Leigh Hunt preserved and illustrated this distinction from a wide range of poets.

[1] Characteristically Wordsworth, in his celebrated preface, illustrated what he meant by Imagination, not from his friend's poetry, but his own. Upon the line " Over his own sweet voice the stock-dove broods," he thus comments: " The stock-dove is said to *coo*, a sound well imitating the note of the bird ; but by the intervention of the metaphor *broods*, the affections are called in by the imagination to assist in marking the manner in which the bird reiterates and prolongs her soft note, as if herself delighting to listen to it, and participatory of a still and quiet satisfaction, like that which may be supposed inseparable from the continuous process of incubation."

2

Mr Ruskin, in the second volume of *Modern Painters* (p. 163), turned aside from an elaborate disquisition upon Imagination in painting to speak of poetry. " The Fancy," he says, " sees the outside, and so is able to give a portrait of the outside, clear, brilliant, and full of detail ; the Imagination sees the heart and inner nature, and makes them felt, but is often obscure, mysterious, and interrupted in its giving of outer detail." And then follows a remarkable parallel between the flower passage in *Lycidas* and that in the *Winter's Tale*, greatly to the disadvantage of the former.

It will be remembered that the passage from *Lycidas* is printed with marginal notes, as follows :—

"Bring the rathe primrose that forsaken dies,	*Imagination.*
The tufted crow-toe, and pale jessamine,	*Nugatory.*
The white pink, and the pansy freaked with jet,	*Fancy.*
The glowing violet,	*Imagination.*
The musk-rose, and the well-attir'd woodbine,	*Fancy and vulgar.*

With cowslips wan that hang
    the pensive head,   *Imagination.*
And every flower that sad em-
    broidery wears."   *Mixed.*

Then follows the passage from the *Winter's Tale* :—

              " O Proserpina,
For the flowers now, that, frighted, thou let'st fall
From Dis's waggon ! daffodils,
That come before the swallow dares, and take
The winds of March with beauty ; violets, dim,
But sweeter than the lids of Juno's eyes,
Or Cytherea's breath ; pale primroses,
That die unmarried, ere they can behold
Bright Phœbus in his strength, a malady
Most incident to maids."

And then comes this criticism :

" Observe how the imagination in these last lines goes into the very inmost soul of every flower, after having touched them all at first with that heavenly timidness, the shadow of Proserpine's, and gilded them with celestial gathering, and never stops on their spots or their bodily shape ; while Milton sticks in the stains upon them and puts us off with that unhappy freak of jet in the very flower that, without this bit of paper-staining, would have been the most precious to us of all. ' There is pansies, that's for thoughts.' "

I do not know whether this comparison has ever been the subject of adverse comment : I have often heard it praised. To me, I confess, it seems a compendium of all the faults that a critic of poetry should avoid : waywardness, preciosity, inattention, and the uncritical use of critical labels. In the first place the critic has ignored what is of the first consequence, the motive of the two pieces, and has treated them as parallel flower-passages from a volume of elegant extracts; whereas no criticism can be to the point that does not recognize that Milton's flowers are being gathered for a funeral, and Shakespeare's are not to be gathered at all; they are visionary spring flowers, seen in glory through the autumn haze. Without going at length through each passage it is worth noticing that Shakespeare's lines about the primrose are open to precisely the same censure, no more and no less, as Mr Ruskin accords to Milton's pansy. The epithet "pale" is very far from "going into the very inmost soul" of the primrose, which is a hardy flower, and not in the least anæmic; it "sticks in the stains" upon the surface as much as the "freaked with jet";

and this, again, so far from being "unhappy," gives the reason why the pansy was chosen for the hearse among the flowers that "sad embroidery wear." A second point to notice concerns the lines that are marked "nugatory." Both Shakespeare and Milton had the instinct to see that just as, on the one hand, a flower-passage must not be a mere catalogue, so, on the other, each item must not be unduly emphasized. And so we find that, while Milton has his "tufted crow-toe and pale jessamine," and his "well-attir'd woodbine" to make up the bunch, Shakespeare also has his

> "Bold oxlips, and
> The crown-imperial, lilies of all kinds,
> The flower-de-luce being one!"

a "nugatory" passage which Mr Ruskin omits from his quotation. So much, then, for the contrast of Imagination and Fancy, which critics might now be content to let die.

In resuming what has been said about the two great characteristics of the poetical mind, its passion and its imagination, it may be useful to illustrate from the picture that our great dramatist has drawn of the poetical character in the person of Macbeth. Macbeth, indeed, was a poet without a conscience; but that circumstance is to the advantage of our illustration, since we shall not be able to confuse his morality with his poetry. There are several points that may be noticed.

1. First, though on this much stress must not be laid, we observe Macbeth's power of summoning up, and vividly objectifying impressions of sense. He sees an air-drawn dagger. He hears a voice say, "Sleep no more."

2. Secondly, and this is fundamental, we remark the passionate intensity with which he realizes whatever comes before him, his own states of mind, or events that happen, and sees them in all their attendant circumstances and consequences. No fact that at all interests him remains a barren fact to him, and most facts

do interest him. When he is contemplating the death of Duncan he appreciates thoroughly and entirely all that is involved in that death :—

> "He's here in double trust :
> First, as I am his kinsman, and his subject,
> Strong both against the deed ; then, as his host,
> Who should against his murderer shut the door,
> Not bear the knife myself. Besides, this Duncan
> Hath borne his faculties so meek, hath been
> So clear in his great office, that his virtues
> Will plead like angels, trumpet-tongued, against
> The deep damnation of his taking-off."

So he goes from point to point, realizing as he goes. Even more striking is the way in which he is moved after the murder by Duncan's untroubled condition, thoroughly appreciating it :—

> "Duncan is in his grave ;
> After life's fitful fever, he sleeps well ;
> Treason has done his worst : nor steel, nor poison,
> Malice domestic, foreign levy, nothing,
> Can touch him further !"

Or consider the passage at the end of the play, where he is contemplating his own deserted state :—

> "I have liv'd long enough ; my way of life
> Is fall'n into the sear, the yellow leaf ;

> And that which should accompany old age,
> As honour, love, obedience, troops of friends,
> I must not look to have ; but, in their stead,
> Curses, not loud, but deep, mouth-honour, breath,
> Which the poor heart would fain deny, but dare not."

Especially characteristic here of the poet seems to me the pause on the idea of curses, to realize them, before going further, " curses, not *loud*, but *deep*."

3. In the third place, we remark that, as Macbeth realizes with such vividness and such emotion the qualities of everything that appeals to him, so one thing is always suggesting another with similar qualities :—

> "Then comes my fit again ; I had else been perfect ;
> Whole as the *marble*, founded as the *rock*,
> As broad and general as the casing *air* ;
> But now I am cabin'd, cribb'd, confined."

When the ghostly voice that he hears, the echo of his own imaginative mind, suggests to him the terrible thought that he has murdered not the king only, but Sleep, the greatest friend of man, he is at once absorbed in the thought of all the wonder and mystery of sleep, which he draws out into a long string of images; forgetting all about the business he had been engaged in, and the bloody daggers in his hand, until his practical wife in blank amazement breaks in with, " What do you mean ? " No one, again, is likely to forget the desolate images under which he sums up his idea of the worthlessness and meaninglessness of human life :

> " Life's but a walking shadow ; a poor player,
> That struts and frets his hour upon the stage,
> And then is seen no more : it is a tale
> Told by an idiot, full of sound and fury,
> Signifying nothing."

4. I would point out, further, as a frequent trait of the poetic nature, Macbeth's simplicity ; shown partly by his interest in his own moods ; for example, in such sayings as " False face must hide what the false heart doth know "; more curiously in his speculation why he could not say "Amen " when the groom he was about to murder said, " God bless us "; most curiously in his irritation at ghost-walking :—

> " The times have been
> That, when the brains were out, the man would die,

And there an end ; but now they rise again,
With twenty mortal murders on their crowns,
And push us from our stools ; this is more strange
Than such a murder is."

5. Finally, though in this I am trespassing
on a subject which I hope to discuss in a second
lecture, we cannot but observe Macbeth's extra-
ordinary talent for expression.   I will give but
one instance.   Shakespeare, whether by design
or chance, has reserved for him what is, perhaps,
the most remarkable presentment in literature of
the phenomenon of falling night—

" Light thickens,"

an expression which gives not only the fact of
growing darkness, but also its qualities.

The picture of the poetical nature that
Shakespeare has given us in Macbeth is con-
siderably heightened if by the side of it we add
for contrast his Richard II.   Without working
out the parallel in any detail, it will be enough
to call attention to two points.   In the first
place, Richard has no imagination in the sense
which we have seen reason to give to that term ;

he has no intuition into the scope and meaning and consequences of human actions. Compare, for instance, with Macbeth's picture of old age, Richard's picture of a dethroned king :—

> "I'll give my jewels for a set of beads,
> My gorgeous palace for a hermitage ;
> My gay apparel for an almsman's gown,
> My figured goblets for a dish of wood ;
> My sceptre for a palmer's walking staff,
> My subjects for a pair of carved saints ;
> And my large kingdom for a little grave," &c.

The points in the picture which rouse Richard's emotion, and which he sets out before us, are all merely superficial; never once does he touch the real heart of the matter. The other noticeable thing is that Richard is much less interested in persons or events than in his feelings about them, and then only in such as are lamentable; and perhaps, it would be true to add, less in the lamentable feelings than in the pathetic language in which they can be expressed. He "hammers out" a simile as though it was an end in itself, and is moved by a curious phrase so as almost to forget his troubles. In the coronation scene, after Richard has cast down the looking-glass with the words,

> " How soon my sorrow hath destroyed my face,"

Bolingbroke, with all a practical man's contempt of play-acting and rhetoric, satirically replies :—

> " The shadow of your sorrow hath destroyed
> The shadow of your face,"

whereupon Richard is at once arrested :—

> " Say that again !
> The shadow of my sorrow ! ha ! let's see ! "

Could there be a more vivid portrait of the " minor poet " or sentimentalist ?

EXPRESSION IN POETRY.

IN the foregoing lecture I ventured an attempt
to investigate the constant qualities of the
poetical mind; in this I wish to consider what
are, speaking generally, the means at the poet's
disposal for conveying his passion and his
imaginative vision to his hearers. For of poets,
as of the rest of us, it may be said that—

> "if our virtues
> Did not go forth of us, 'twere all alike
> As if we had them not."

A "mute" Milton would certainly be "inglori-
ous"; he would also be useless: would he be
conceivable? Undoubtedly we can distinguish
in thought the divine vision from the divine
faculty which gives it expression, but is this

distinction anything more than logical? May
not the truth be that a poet expresses more
than the rest of the world because he sees
more, and like the rest of the world can express up to the limit of his vision? Our tutors
and governors, when we were children, used to
receive with well-grounded suspicion our not
infrequent excuse for muteness, "I know, but
I can't explain"; and it is equally probable
that in poets the vision brings its own inter-
pretative faculty. It is beyond dispute that
the poets who have had the finest things to
say are those who have said them most finely.
If we take those passages which Matthew Arnold
once suggested as touchstones of high poetic
quality, and attempt to distinguish in them what
is form from what is substance, we shall find the
task impossible.

> "Wilt thou upon the high and giddy mast
> Seal up the ship boy's eyes, and rock his brains
> In cradle of the rude, imperious surge? . . ."

Is there here one word not necessary for the

picture it presents, one epithet we could obelize as inserted in the interests of mere style? "High" is not enough without "giddy," because the poet wishes to suggest the incredibleness, from a landsman's point of view, of sleep under such conditions; "rude" and "imperious" are both required to suggest the power of sleep which can ignore so savage a tyrant, nay, use him for her purposes, for it is the tossing that rocks the boy to sleep. We may then lay it down that, just as when we have reached our maturity and have something to say, the contents of our mind are, as a matter of fact, conveyed into our language with no appreciable loss, so that what we say is a faithful transcription of what we think, and our friends are seldom at a loss for our meaning; so the poet's mood, by an even surer instinct, chooses for itself language which effectually conveys his passion or imaginative vision. The mystery in the relation of poetical vision to poetical expression is the prime mystery of all human speech; it is a mystery, and we cannot get behind it; but it is not greater in the case of poets than with ordinary men and women. The great difference, from which all else depends, lies behind expression, in the texture of the poet's thought and feeling. I know that it is the fashion of the moment to make more of the distinction between artist and amateur than of that between poet and poetaster. I am, however, not denying that the poet is an artist. The instinct I speak of is an artistic instinct. Nor would I deny that every poet must serve an apprenticeship to his art, and improve by practice his gift of expression. It is to be hoped that even those of us who talk prose improve by practice. My contention is merely that when the poem is written and before us, it will take rank, supposing it to be a true poem, by the thing said, and that it will be found impossible to distinguish the substance from the form. A very simple consideration will show the truth of this position.

Why is it that the *Idylls of the King* and the *In Memoriam* contain so many passages that the world will quite willingly let die? If the chief thing in poetry were the style, one part of these poems would be as good as another, for the style is uniform throughout. The answer, in all such cases, is that "soul is form and doth the body make." What is wanting in the weak places of these great poems is the soul, the poetic vision and enthusiasm, the absence of which no style can compensate.

That being premised, we may go on to consider the most general means which the poet does, as a matter of fact, employ to convey to us his emotion.

1. Poetry is essentially passionate, and its passion requires a heightened mode of expression. In our literature this is supplied by metre. At its lowest, metre is, what Coleridge called it, "a stimulant of the attention." At the very least, it cuts off what is said from ordinary surroundings and raises it to an ideal

plane ; so that if what is said in metre be
commonplace, its commonplaceness becomes at
once more apparent.   Hence bad verse is more
intolerable than bad prose.   But further, metre
being not only rhythm but regulated rhythm,
it is excellently adapted as a medium for poetry,
which is not only emotion but, as Wordsworth
said, "recollected emotion"; not wild passion,
but passion conceived of as something in itself
precious, which the poet wishes to impart to
others.   The poet desires to rouse not any
emotion, but some one emotion in particular.
Hence various emotions find their fit expression
in appropriate metres.   It is not by idle chance
or mere caprice that *Paradise Lost* is written
in iambic verse and Shelley's *Ode to a Skylark*
in trochaics.   Even in metres which appear to
be least bound by rule, such as the choruses
in *Samson Agonistes*, it will be found on in-
vestigation that a reason underlies the apparent
vagary.   It is with these rhythms as with the
wheels in Ezekiel's vision : " To the place

whither the head looked they followed it, for the spirit of a living creature was in them."

But although every poem must be written not in rhythm only, but in metre, it is possible while preserving the framework of metre to vary the rhythm by changes in pause and accent. Hood's *Eugene Aram* and Rossetti's *Blessed Damosel* are written in the same metre, but the differences in rhythm are so great that the one poem never for a moment suggests the other. Similarly Tennyson's blank verse does not recall Milton's. And within the same poem a writer will vary his rhythm, partly for the sake of the variety, but also in order to produce special effects. Some such effects are fairly obvious and will be found generalised in ancient and modern treatises, like Horace's *Ars Poetica* and Pope's *Essay on Criticism* :—

> "When Ajax strives some rock's vast weight to throw
> The line too labours and the words move slow, &c."

Other effects can only be recognized when the poet's artistic sense has achieved them. Thus

in Tennyson's *Idylls of the King*, we have, on
the ground-plan of his unrhymed five-accent
line, effects as markedly different as the follow-
ing, in each of which the rhythm helps to
express the action described :—

"So dark a forethought roll'd about his brain,
  As on a dull day in an Ocean cave
  The blind wave feeling round his long sea-hall
  In silence."
                "Gareth loosed the stone
  From off his neck; then in the mere beside
  Tumbled it; oilily bubbled up the mere."

Almost any page of *Paradise Lost* will supply
examples of greater or less subtlety.   There is
an easy contrast for instance between the description of Satan's mounting to the roof of
Hell, where the rhythm is almost dactylic :—

                "Some times
  He scours the right-hand coast, some times the left,
  Now shaves with level wing the deep, then soars
  Up to the fiery concave, towering high."

and the succession of strong accents in the description of his flight down to the earth from
heaven :—

"*Down right into the world's first region throws*
His flight precipitant and winds with ease
Through the pure marble air his oblique ray
Amongst innumerable stars,"

while the rhythm follows with even more delicate faithfulness the other motions described.

2. A second great means employed by English poetry to express emotion is rhyme. Rhyme, as much as metre, is a mode of heightening expression, a stimulant to the attention. Attempts have been made from time to time to abandon the use of rhyme altogether, as a relic of barbarism. Campion, who himself used rhyme to delightful effect, wrote a treatise to prove its "unaptness for poesy"; and even Milton in his old age wrote a preface to his epic in which he disparaged it, not only as a "troublesome bondage in heroic poem," which no doubt it is; and not only as "the invention of a barbarous age to set off wretched matter and lame metre," as perhaps it was; but as "a thing of itself to all judicious ears trivial, and of no true musical delight." Thus the

author of *Paradise Lost* turned his back on
the author of *Lycidas*. And yet still later in
his life Milton's true poetic instinct once more
vindicated rhyme against this critical judgment
by using it to " set off metre," that was far from
lame, in the choruses of *Samson*.

> " All is best, though we oft doubt
>   What th' unsearchable dispose
> Of highest wisdom brings about
>   And ever best found in the close.
> Oft he seems to hide his face
>   But unexpectedly returns,
> And to his faithful champion hath in place
>   Bore witness gloriously whence Gaza mourns,
> And all that band them to resist
>   His uncontrollable intent.
> His servants he with new acquist
>   Of true experience from this great event
> With peace and consolation hath dismist
>   And calm of mind, all passion spent."

Is the rhyme in this fine passage otiose and
trivial ? No one can fail to observe what variety
it lends to the chorus by ringing the changes
on all the chief vowel sounds, or how it marks
sections of the thought ; first the text, then the
illustration, then the moral. The second sec-

tion, indeed, runs on into the third quatrain of rhymes ; but by that slight irregularity the ode is bound together, and the ear kept on the alert, until the full close, for the chime that is sure to come.

3. These things, then, metre and rhyme, being granted to the poet as two ingredients of his magic cauldron, by means of which he is to conjure up the mood or scene that he desires to set before us, we come to the third, his use of words, and proceed to enquire whether there are any principles governing the use of language peculiar to poetry. Here it must be remembered that all a critic can do is to analyse more or less successfully what methods have actually been employed by this poet and that for the production of their effects. There is no one poetic method, just as there is no separate poetic vocabulary. Every new poet will achieve his new result in a new way, which he will find the easier and also the harder for the enterprise of his predecessors. There are, how-

ever, two or three artistic principles of universal application which call for notice. The first is, that the poem must have an atmosphere of its own ; or, to change the metaphor, the words must be all in the same key. Now, no mere poetical joinery can achieve such a result as this. Unless the words are generated by "thoughts that breathe," they will have no life in them, and no natural and inevitable relation to each other. For an example, take a quatrain from Gray's beautiful sonnet upon his friend West :—

> "These ears, alas ! for other notes repine ;
>   A different object do these eyes require ;
>   My lonely anguish melts no heart but mine,
>   And in my breast the imperfect joys expire."

These lines were chosen by Wordsworth in his famous Preface to point the moral that the language of poetry differs in no respect from that of prose when it is well written. The moral they really point is a different one. Their tone is unique ; it is unlike that of any other elegy in the language. The poet's instinct has guided him securely to express his own special emotion, and to avoid any word " of dissonant mood from his complaint." Whether the words might be classed as prosaic or poetical he has not stopped to enquire. If a poetaster had been writing the sonnet, he would have avoided what would have seemed to him so tame an expression as " the imperfect joys expire." But how absolutely right it is, in its place and for its purpose. Again, what but genius could have conceived the reticence of the two epithets "other" and "different"? It should be clear, then, that one principle governing the use of words in poetry is that every poem must have an atmosphere of its own ; it must be in a definite mode, to which the poet's emotion will guide him surely. The poet's passion may be any one of a myriad moods, for the heart of man is infinite, and the special quality of the particular passion will show itself in the quality of the words. We shall feel it in them, even though we are not able to describe it. When people say "this is genuine poetry," what they often mean is that a passionate mood has succeeded, by the poet's instinct, in condensing itself into words, and in reading the words they distinguish the passion. Consider, for a second example, a stanza in Wordsworth's *Solitary Reaper* :—

> "Will no one tell me what she sings?
>   Perhaps the plaintive numbers flow
> For old, unhappy, far-off things,
>   And battles long ago."

If we take these lines to pieces, we may be tempted to say it is the prosiest verse ever written ; "old," "unhappy," "far-off," are words of an everyday vocabulary, and "Will no one tell me what she sings?" might almost occur in any drawing-room conversation. But if we are content not to take the passage to pieces, if we are content to receive it and let it make its own impression as a whole, we must acknowledge it to be a perfect rendering of the effect on the poet's mind of the wild, vague, sad Highland music. A good proof of poetical adequacy is that such lines cannot be paraphrased.

It is an interesting experience to take up a Shakespeare and remark how the speeches, apart from their merely grammatical sense, are all pitched in a certain key, and make on us the impression of a definite mood. Take, for an instance, the familiar lines of Demetrius in *A Midsummer Night's Dream*, after the troubles and misunderstandings of the night are over and he is looking back upon them :—

> " These things seem small and undistinguishable,
> Like far-off mountains turned into clouds."

The mere grammatical sense, if the words were paraphrased, would not be striking, but the words themselves convey—who can tell how?—the wondering reverie of a man still only half awake*. It is even more interesting to study

---

* It is noticeable that those short passages in which Shakespeare describes a sunrise all take colour from the circumstances of the *dramatis personæ*. Shakespeare has not a pigeon-hole for sunrises from which he draws indiscriminately at need. To the ghost in *Hamlet* the morning comes as the twilight of

with the same view the pictures of landscape in the works of the great masters. Landscape, of course, is far from being a fixed quantity. The poet, indeed, paints what he *sees;* but that means he paints what *he* sees ; and in painting he paints his own mood, even though he does not necessarily mean to do so. How definite is the mood of the concluding passage of Keats' *Ode to Autumn :—*

> " Hedge-crickets sing, and now, with treble soft,
> The redbreast whistles from a garden croft,
> And gathering swallows twitter in the skies."

The tone of the words is of a somewhat meagre joy. All the verbs contain the vowel *i,* the thinnest of vowels. The poet seems to say: " The glory of the year is departing, but it is not yet gone, let us make the best of what

night, which is his day, and so he expresses it by reference to the paling light of the glow-worm :—

> "The glow-worm shews the matin to be near,
> And 'gins to pale his uneffectual fire."

A remarkable contrast to the lively image of Horatio :—

> "But look, the morn in russet mantle clad
> Walks o'er the dew of yon high eastern hill!"

remains." He does not say that ; he gives but
a hint of it in the gathering of the swallows,
and for the rest sings the best *Jubilate* he can.
But the mood is unmistakable. Contrast with
it as celebrated a picture of Autumn, that by
Crabbe, at the end of *Delay has Danger*:—

> " He saw the wind upon the water blow;
>   Far to the left he saw the huts of men,
>   Half hid in mist that hung upon the fen ;
>   Before him swallows, gathering for the sea,
>   Took their short flights, and twittered on the lea;
>   And near the bean-sheaf stood, the harvest done,
>   And slowly blackened in the sickly sun."

There is only one epithet there which very
definitely fixes the key of the passage, the epithet
"sickly"; and I am not sure that it does not
a little force the note, and spoil the harmony.
Apart from that there is nothing ; and yet the
mood is unmistakable. It is a mood of deep
dejection. You can hear it in every line, even
in such a line as

> " He saw the wind upon the water blow,"

which contains no epithet, and yet makes you
shiver. I need not, perhaps, further illustrate

this first principle, that given a mood of emotion, it can and will find means of expressing itself unmistakably.

It may, however, be well to illustrate the fact that the poet's instinct may not always secure the most adequate expression at the first attempt. In Trinity College, Cambridge, there is preserved a manuscript of certain of Milton's minor poems which shows that he achieved some of his most consummate results by a series of experiments, each bringing him nearer to his goal. One of the most marvellous lines in the *Comus* comes in a passage where the Lady lost in the dark wood falls a prey to vague midnight fancies, and says :—

> "A thousand fantasies
> Begin to throng into my memory
> Of calling shapes, and beckoning shadows dire,
> *And airy tongues that syllable men's names*
> On sands and shores and desert wildernesses."

For the line in italics Milton had originally written "And airy tongues that lure night-wanderers"; but how vastly better did his second thoughts convey his sense. "Syllable" is a word exquisitely fitted for his purpose. Being pure sound, it suggests the idea of words being uttered that are mere sounds, words said by "airy tongues" with no intelligence behind them, words said clearly and carefully as by a child who does not know the meaning of what he is saying. The manuscripts of Shelley and Coleridge tell a like tale. And even where manuscripts are not to be had, it is often possible, by comparing the several editions of a poem, to see how, by a slight touch here and there, the poet has succeeded in conveying his meaning to us more perfectly. Let me give two examples from Tennyson. In the first edition of the *Princess*, the first line of that exquisite song, "Home they brought her warrior dead," appeared as "Home they brought him, slain with spears." Clearly the poet perceived that he had been trying to convey too much : the kind of battle in which the warrior fell was really unimportant for his purpose ; the important fact was the fact of death. So he moved the word *dead* to the most emphatic place in the line, and implied the death in battle by the word *warrior*. The other example I would adduce is the first line of *Tithonus*, which, when it first appeared in the *Cornhill Magazine*, ran :—

"Ay me, ay me, the woods decay and fall."

This was subsequently altered into its present form,

"The woods decay, the woods decay, and fall,"

a much better line under the circumstances ; because the repetition of the clause "the woods decay" creates a pause before the words "and fall," which are the words of most emphasis, and are thus thrown into greater prominence. Tithonus, too, had decayed, like the leaves ; unlike them, he could not come altogether to an end. It is interesting also to notice that while some poets are thus able to recollect their emotion and improve by revision the expression of it, others totally lack this power. A striking instance was William Morris.

A second great artistic principle in the poetical use of language is the axiom laid down by Coleridge that a poet should "paint to the imagination"; by which is meant that the poet should never, in describing objects, labour to accumulate detail, but find some way of summoning up his picture before our eyes at a stroke. This principle, coming from a poet, reminds one, to compare great things with small, of the explanations given by conjurors of their tricks. "That," they say, "is how it's done." How to do it is a different matter. But that it is really done so, we may convince ourselves by taking examples. Matthew Arnold among the touchstones of poetry, to which I have already referred, included those lines of Milton about the Rape of Proserpine,

> "Which cost Ceres all that pain
> To seek her through the world."

Who but a poet of the first rank would have dared that simple touch, "*all that* pain"; how effective it is upon the mind of the instructed reader, for whom alone Milton wrote ; what accumulation of epithet could produce a tenth part of the effect ? Whatever we have read in old poets at once leaps to memory.

This principle of calling in the reader's imagination to fill out the poet's outline helps us to understand why poets are so ready to compare one thing with another. The process is a kind of hypnotism ; the poet makes a suggestion and the reader at once sees the picture*. A simple and very effective instance is Tennyson's comparison of the pallor of the wounded King's face to the fading moon—

> "All his face was white
> And colourless, and like the wither'd moon
> Smote by the fresh beam of the springing East."

The painting of landscape in the poetry of

---

* It is not merely physical resemblances that are best indicated by imagery. Thoughts and sentiments are often poetically enforced by a comparison, which in pure reason is not to the point.

> " Weep no more, nor sigh, nor groan,
>   Sorrow calls no time that's gone;
>   *Violets pluck'd the sweetest rain*
>   *Makes not fresh or grow again.*"

this century owes a great deal to this illustrative method. It is plain that the most painful and literal accuracy could not give the picture of autumn leaves driven before the wind so fully and effectively as Shelley's fine image—

"Like ghosts from an enchanter fleeing,"

or the picture of the sudden thrusting and thronging of spring buds in hedgerows and garden beds so well as another image in the same poem—

"Driving sweet buds like flocks to feed in air."

In still higher poetry we may see the principle at work in such a piece as Shakespeare's seventy-third sonnet :—

"That time of year thou mayst in me behold,
    When yellow leaves, or none, or few, do hang
  Upon those boughs which shake against the cold,—
    Bare, ruin'd choirs, where late the sweet birds sang.
  In me thou see'st the twilight of such day,
    As, after sunset, fadeth in the west,
  Which by and by black night doth take away,
    Death's second self, that seals up all in rest.
  In me thou see'st the glowing of such fire,
    That on the ashes of his youth doth lie,

As the death-bed whereon it must expire,
    Consum'd with that which it was nourish'd by.
This thou perceiv'st, which makes thy love more strong,
To love that well, which thou must leave ere long."

The root-thought in this sonnet is that the coming on of age makes the friend's love stronger, because the time is short. The picture of age is brought before us, however, not directly, but by three pictorial comparisons : first, to the dying of the year, then to the dying of each day, then to the dying down of a fire ; each supplying some vivid detail which applies with special poignancy to the lover's case—and the first especially reminding us by reference to the "ruined choirs" that the aged lover is also the poet.

In conclusion, it may be noted that there are certain qualities of individual words of which poets, above all other writers, are careful to take advantage. The poet is alive to the associations of words. In the line quoted above from Gray,

"A different object do these eyes require,"

it is plain that the word *require* is used with
a reminiscence of such a Virgilian line as

"Amissos longo socios sermone *requirunt*,"

and brings with it the wistfulness of the Latin.
Milton and Tennyson are especially happy in
such learned use of words.   Further, the poet
can, and constantly does, take advantage of the
actual sound of the words themselves.   The
device of alliteration has passed in English from
being part of the mechanism of all poetry, an
initial rhyme, into a means of producing special
effects ; effects as various as the quality of the
several letters.   It needs no enforcing that in
such a phrase as Milton's

"Behemoth, biggest born of earth,"

the repeated effort to form the labial helps the
imagination to an impression of bigness, while in
another line of his—

"The world of waters wide and deep,"

or " wallowing unwieldy," the open effect of the
three w's helps the all-abroadness of the idea.

So liquids minister to a verse of their liquidity, and sibilants can soothe a verse to sleep as well as a child. What goes commonly by the name of *onomatopœia* is a step beyond this. Here actual sounds in nature are more or less suggested. Some words, such as *murmuring*, are themselves onomatopœic in origin ; others have come to be so by chance, or are compelled into such service by the poet. Examples are *drizzling, trickling, tumbling, noise, cry*, all of which are to be found in the stanza of the *Faerie Queene* describing the cave of Morpheus.

> "And more to lull him in his slumber soft,
> A trickling stream from high rock tumbling down,
> And ever-drizzling rain upon the loft,
> Mixt with a murmuring wind, much like the sown
> Of swarming bees, did cast him in a swoun ;
> No other noise, nor people's troublous cries,
> As still are wont to annoy the wallèd town,
> Might here be heard ; but careless Quiet lies
> Wrapt in eternal silence far from enemies."

Beyond *onomatopœia*, again, we have in certain poets, but by no means all, the power of suggesting by words not sound only but motion.

Keats succeeds occasionally in this sort of cinematographic effect, *e.g.*, in his description of a gust of wind coming and going.

> "Save for one gradual solitary gust,
> Which comes upon the silence and dies off
> As if the ebbing air had but one wave."

Much of the effect of this passage is due to the emphatic monosyllable "comes," which gives the impression of suddenness. Keats puts it to much the same service in his description of the moon breaking from a cloud. And much of the effect of Tennyson's *Crossing the Bar*, one of his most admirable pictures of motion, depends upon the monosyllabic verbs.

> "May there be no moaning of the bar
>   When I put out to sea,
> But such a tide as *moving* seems asleep
>   Too full for sound or foam,
> When that which *drew* out of the boundless deep,
>   *Turns* again home."

I will conclude with a passage, written by one who was himself a master of the poetic craft, analysing the suggestiveness of the sound effects in a couplet of Coleridge's *Christabel* :—

"The brands were flat, the brands were dying,
   Amid their own white ashes lying."

" Here the cold vowels *a, i, o* are the only
ones which are openly sounded, and of these
a is repeated five times, and *i* three times, the
e in the short *the* preceding, as it does, the long
syllable *brand* is scarcely heard; the ear is
wholly occupied with the eight cold vowels
which occur in the long syllables of the eight
feet that constitute these lines. The only effect
of warmth is a very slight one, produced by the
rapid succession of the consonants *b, r* and *n, d*
in the word *brand*. Again, there is an effect of
weight conveyed by the word *brand*, and to this
effect we are invited to attend, by the repetition
of it, and by the first juxtaposition and contrast
of this word with other words conveying the
notion of softness and lightness ; finally the
two ideas of lightness and weight are united,
and the effect completed by the word *amid*, in
which the sound passing through the soft *m* and
its indistinct vowels, concludes in a heavy *d* ;

and completes to a delicate ear and a prepared mind, the entire picture of the weighty and smouldering brands, sunken through the light mass of ashes which remains after their undisturbed combustion*."

* Coventry Patmore in a review of Tennyson's *Princess*, quoted in Patmore's *Life*, i. 106.

www.ingramcontent.com/pod-product-compliance
Ingram Content Group UK Ltd.
Pitfield, Milton Keynes, MK11 3LW, UK
UKHW042148280225
455719UK00001B/202